Dedicated to all of God's precious children
in our world waiting to be adopted.

He hears and listens to your prayers.

Always believe in your dreams
and never give up.

A portion of the proceeds of this book
will be donated to children with Autism.

Penny Puppy
and
The Perfect Parents

Written by Debbie Wood

Illustrated by Theresa Stites

If you believe, you will receive whatever you ask for in prayer.

Once upon a time there was a beautiful puppy named Penny. She had pretty brown hair which she always kept tied up in bows and beautiful green eyes. Penny was five years old and she was always smiling. Penny had a smile for everyone and was always the first one to make everyone laugh.

Her favorite saying was

"Turn that frown upside down".

Turn that frown upside down

It seemed as if Penny had a wonderful life but there were a couple of things in Penny's life that some people might think were sad.

These were the only things that sometimes made Penny's heart feel blue.

Penny had a very special friend named Jesus who lived in her heart. She couldn't see him but she knew he was there because of how she felt inside.

Penny knew that if she asked Jesus and truly believed that someday her wishes would come true.

Penny lived with a foster mommy and father and many other children. Her first wish was that she would get a mommy and daddy of her very own.

Her second wish was for someone to love her even though her legs weren't perfect and she needed to be in a wheelchair.

Penny would smile as she sat by her bedroom window and watched her friends play games outside. She would daydream about running to catch a ball or playing hide and go seek. Penny's biggest dreams were about having a real mommy who would read her stories at bedtime, take her to birthday parties, and go shopping for pretty dresses and dollies she could play with.

Sometimes that's when her heart would start to hurt but Penny kept believing and smiling because she knew that someday her prayers would be answered.

Penny just kept on making people smile and was always there to lend a helping hand. This made her feel good inside and that's why her friends called her "Perfect Penny".

Believe Love

Jesus

Pray Hope

One day when Penny came home from school her foster mommy told her that she had a very special surprise for her. Penny couldn't even imagine what it could be. So many things raced through her mind. As Penny came into the living room there sat a beautiful woman with brown hair and green eyes. She was so pretty and next to her was a very handsome man. They were both smiling happy smiles.

Penny was so surprised that she hardly noticed the special chair that the nice lady was sitting in.

"Well hello Penny, we've been waiting to meet you for a very long time.", the lady said sweetly. Penny couldn't believe her ears. Her voice trembled and she spoke...

"Why would you want to meet me?
I'm no one special."

Penny never smiled so big.

"I've been asking my special friend, Jesus for a perfect mommy and daddy and now you're here!"

Just then Patrick walked over and lifted Penny right out of her chair and placed her on Patty's lap. Penny and Patty held each other. It was then that Penny knew that her dreams had come true.

She was going to have perfect parents with perfect hearts.

With a smile the lady said "My name is Patty and this is my husband, Patrick".

For such a long time we've been praying for the perfect little girl. When we heard about you we had to come right down here to meet you. Right when you came into the room, I knew that my prayers had been answered but I'm not perfect. I have to use my special chair to get around too.

Would this be okay with you?"

If you'd like Jesus as your best friend!

John 3:16
"For God so loved the world that he gave his only begotten son that whosoever believeth in Him shall not perish but have everlasting life."

www.ingramcontent.com/pod-product-compliance
Lightning Source LLC
Chambersburg PA
CBHW082249300426
44110CB00039B/2488